ROOT TO FRUIT

COMING OUT OF THE
HIDDEN ROOT SYSTEMS THAT TRIP YOU UP

DONNA BIANCHI

Copyright © 2020 Donna Bianchi

ISBN: 979-8-9856294-1-5

ROOT TO FRUIT:

How To End Negative Life Patterns and Emotionally Reset All rights reserved.

No part of this publication may be reproduced, distributed, or transmitted in any form or by any means, including photocopying, recording, or other electronic or mechanical methods, without the prior written permission of the publisher, except in the case of brief quotations embodied in critical reviews and certain other non-commercial uses permitted by copyright law.

Donna Bianchi First Edition 2020

Dedicated to The Father, Son, and Holy Spirit who is The Lord Jesus Christ who wants His people healed.

TABLE OF CONTENTS

INTRODUCTION VII

CHAPTER 1 - ROOTS TO FRUITS 1

CHAPTER 2 - HOW DO YOU FIND THE ROOT OF A NEGATIVE PATTERN IN YOUR LIFE? 3

CHAPTER 3 - WHY ARE YOU HERE? 7

CHAPTER 4 - JUDGING YOUR PARENTS: A CASE STUDY 9

CHAPTER 5 - PRAYER TO END BITTER ROOT EXPECTATIONS 15

CHAPTER 6 - INNER VOWS 17

CHAPTER 7 - PRAYER TO BREAK INNER VOWS 21

CHAPTER 8 - REJECTION 23

CHAPTER 9 - PRAYING THROUGH REJECTING YOUR OWN SPIRIT 25

CHAPTER 10 - IDENTITY ISSUES 29

CHAPTER 11 - SOUL TIES 33

CHAPTER 12 - SAMPLE PRAYERS TO BREAK SOUL TIES 35

CONCLUSION 43

INTRODUCTION

I designed this book to give you a do-it-yourself paradigm of the four essential infrastructure pieces that all inner healing builds on.

These four pillars are:

1. Fruit and root—or judgments and bitter root expectations;

2. Shame and identity issues;

3. Inner vows; and

4. Soul ties.

Once you understand these four pillars, you will be able to allow the Holy Spirit to dig deeper into your heart and get more personal with your healing story.

As you allow that more profound entrance into your story, the Lord will show you places where you have been stuck all your life (and probably didn't even realize it) and the way out!

CHAPTER 1

Roots to Fruits

When I was sixteen, I dreamed of becoming a great painter and a great artist.

Chasing that dream, I took a lot of art classes. During my junior year in high school, I had an assignment in art class where we had to use two opposite colors on the color wheel, mix them and make variations, then at the very end, add a third color.

The picture I had in my mind'seye to paint was a side slice, if you will, of a tree, so you saw the tree and all the branches going up, and then you saw the root system like you were looking down through a crosssection of layers of soil.

The exciting thing about that painting was that the roots exactly mirrored the branches. I did that purposely because that is what I saw in my mind.

I used black and white and variations of gray in this painting, even though, technically, I wasn't supposed to use that combination according to the assignment. In the end, I kept looking at it because it needed the third color.

I took a vibrant, deep, red, the color of blood, with a sudden inspiration, and swished up into the branches, coming from the roots, into the shape of a cross. I remember thinking: "Oh my goodness."

It was a prophetic painting, but at that time I had no idea.

I did not remember this painting for many years until a short time ago.

When I did remember it, I realized that even then, God was showing me a critical concept that has become an anchor in what He has called me to do:

If there is bad fruit in your life, there is also a bad root.

We know in the natural realm that the roots of a tree don't always mirror the branches exactly. But in the spiritual and emotional realms, they usually do.

This is a primary truth in inner healing: *fruits match roots.*

If there is something in your life that is persistently not working well (a bad fruit), as a negative pattern, it is because there is a bad root.

And conversely, if something is working successfully in your life (a good fruit), it is because there is a good root.

CHAPTER 2

How Do You Find The Root Of A Negative Pattern In Your Life?

Most negative patterns begin in childhood, between conception and age seven or eight. The negative pattern usually develops because something happened to you during that time.

I get a lot of pushbacks from people when I explain this to them because most people don't have many memories from that time in their lives.

They don't remember the adverse event, and they don't remember responding in a way that sets the negative pattern.

However, even most psychology texts teach that your core personality forms between conception and age seven. How you perceive the world and your behavior patterns become set during this time.

So, whether or not you have concrete memories, your perception of reality during that time becomes the bedrock on which your life is built.

I do a lot of work on in-utero memories as well. People often have a difficult time accepting that they **have** in-utero memories. But there is a large body of work on that topic as well.

Many years ago, a book came out that I recommend for people struggling with the concept called *The Secret Life of The Unborn Child.*

The evidence for in-utero spiritual/emotional wounds is ample, whether you agree with the idea or not. You are a spiritual being, and your spirit is very aware, even in the womb, of what is happening around you.

For instance: A lot of what we know as gender confusion begins in the womb. Many children are born with the persistent thought that they are the wrong sex. Why? Because their parents want a boy or a girl when they are of the opposite sex.

Another way in-utero wounds happen is from the mother using drugs or alcohol during pregnancy. It affects the child not only physically but also spiritually.

When someone is experiencing a persistent, negative pattern, especially one that has persisted throughout their whole life, I look for something that has affected them deeply between conception and age seven or eight.

I want to emphasize that it also takes the Holy Spirit revealing and connecting you to the memory of the incident(s).

A second data point for the formation of negative patterns is simply the Biblical commandment that states: "Honor your father and mother so that your days will be long on the earth in the land that the Lord your God brings you into."

If there is a negative pattern where "things are not going well with you" occurring in your life, it is because you have not honored (or have even dishonored) your father or mother in some area.

Let me give you an example:

I once had a man call me at his wife's insistence. They were Christians, and they were separated and preparing for divorce. He was living in a different town than she was at the time.

I asked him, "What is the problem?"

He answered, "I just can't be faithful to my wife."

I asked him one quick question, "What was your dad like?"

He answered, in a voice heavy with judgment, "My father was very unfaithful to my mother. He was never there," etc., etc., etc.

I said, "There you go. That's the root. Quite simply, you judged your father for being unfaithful, and you are now reaping that judgment. Because you have not honored your father in that area, you have reaped what you have sown and become just like him."

The man was shocked. We prayed through that judgment. He forgave his father for being unfaithful to his mom and asked the Lord to forgive him for judging his father.

When we were done, he said, "You have done more for me in

fifteen minutes than all the psychologists and psychiatrists I've ever been to."

He had spent a lot of money and a lot of time trying to figure this issue out. Quite honestly, I don't know the end of his story. I don't know if he and his wife got back together because I never heard from either one of them again.

This is how negative patterns work. If there is a bad fruit in your life (a negative pattern), there is a bad root. It's usually connected to something your parents did, or did not, do—and the judgment you have made about your parents for this.

This brings us to a third data point, the reaping.

When we judge somebody, the Bible says we who judge become just like what we judge. We exhibit the same negative pattern we've judged in someone else.

Often, our negative pattern is worse than that of the person we judged. Sometimes doubly so. In judging parents, it's a hundred- fold more because of the universal Biblical law—where the sins of the father are visited on the children to the third and fourth generation, growing exponentially with each generation.

To summarize: Bad fruit (negative patterns) means there is a bad root. Usually, this comes from a judgment against our parents (or another wound) from conception to age seven.

CHAPTER 3

Why Are You Here?

The first question I ask most people when they come to me for counseling is: **Why are you here?**

The next is, **What is going on in your life?**

More often than not, the person is in some sort of crisis. They are on the verge of divorce or some other serious life dilemma.

And, they think that situation is the problem.

The truth is, their crisis is NOT the problem. It is merely **the fruit of the root problem.**

The root problem (therefore the REAL problem) is how they have responded to something that happened to them in their past that created the present fruit.

Because a crisis is just that—a crisis, and it is so big and so obvious, it is easy to mistake it for the actual problem.

If it's a divorce or a relationship issue, they are also quick to say it's the other person's problem; "If the other person would just act right, everything would be fine."

Most of the time, the other person is not there, and I answer, "That may be true, but we can't talk with them since they aren't here, we can allow the Lord to work on you."

A critical key here is that we have to ask God to shine His light into this situation because, quite frankly, only **He** can connect your bad fruit to the root that it came from in a way you can understand.

If you're going through a divorce or someone's been unfaithful to you, the next thing I'll say is: "Let's ask the Lord to show you what the root of that is."

Invariably, as the Lord takes people back to the root, they remember that their mother or father had committed adultery. Or, their mother or father had gotten divorced and remarried several times. Sometimes, parents have never married their spouse and the person who comes to me has made judgments against their parents for that.

When the Lord brings that situation and subsequent judgment out, He is quick to show them how this has been a pattern in their life.

Sometimes it's even a generational pattern, often going back for many generations. A generational pattern is also something a person needs to pray through, but more on that later.

Most often, though, it's how the person responded to their parents' actions of infidelity or divorce or other actions. There are many different ways children react to their parents' issues. The Holy Spirit has to show you exactly how you responded to it.

CHAPTER 4

Judging Your Parents: A Case Study

Let's look at a real-life case study on the effects of judging your parents. I am going to use myself as the example.

I went to a private, all-girls Catholic school from kindergarten through high school.

When I went to college (at the University of Tennessee, a public school), it was the first time I was in a mixed school environment— boys and girls combined.

College was five-hundred miles away from home, across the state (I am from Tennessee) near the Great Smoky Mountains.

All of it was a new and very different experience for me.

On the first day of orientation, before my first consultation with my counselor, a young, handsome man walked up to me, introduced himself, and asked me out on a date at the end of the day.

I agreed, and we met after my orientation appointments for a drive into the Great Smoky Mountains.

We drove up into the mountains, stopped at a stream and hiked in the hills. It was a remarkable moment.

All of a sudden, I noticed a gold wedding band on the guy's left hand.

I said, "Are you married?" And he confessed that "Yes," he was. I was just flabbergasted. I had never had anything like that happen to me.

I told him immediately to take me back to the campus.

And that was a scenario that kept repeating itself for almost my whole time in college. Men would ask me out, and it'd turn out that they were married. Not divorced, not separated, or getting divorced. Just married men, one after another, would ask me out.

It wasn't until I went through inner healing counseling when I was in middle age that the Lord showed me the root of that pattern.

Let me explain how this all connects.

I had made the judgment that my father had been unfaithful to my mother with lots of women. I did not have actual, hard evidence of this. Only her reaction to him and him not being home much.

I had made a judgment against my father, "That's how all men are. Unfaithful to their wives."

Once made, it got buried in my memory, and I didn't remember it.

But, the fruit was there. Once buried in my memory, it created an expectation that drew that behavior out of "all men." We call that a "bitter root expectation." That expectation drew married men to me, to be unfaithful to their wives, without me even being aware of it.

Here is an important point: You have to realize it's not just your relationship with your dad or your relationship with your mom that creates your understanding of what men, women, and marriage are. Their relationship with each other begins to paint the picture for you how marriage and relationships are supposed to be between men and women.

Because of what I saw between my parents and because I had a child's incomplete perspective, I made a judgment that all men, not just my father, but all men (because that's what I thought I saw men were like from my father's behavior) are womanizers and cheaters and adulterers.

That created the bitter root expectation (that unconscious expectancy that draws certain, expected behaviors out of people) that that is who/how men were. Because I had that bitter root expectation, that is what I was attracting— unfaithful, womanizing men.

The Bible says in Hebrews 12:15: "Be careful and let no bitter root spring up in you, therefore defiling many." What a bitter root does. If you make a judgment about something you have experienced in childhood, whether you want to or not, it creates an unconscious expectancy in you. Because of this expectancy, you will pull the expected behavior (based on your judgment) out of other people, even if they are not like that.

Here is another example from my own life:

I married young, and I pulled the expectation that men would be unfaithful and womanizers (based on the judgment I had made on my father) out of my first husband. My bitter root pushed buttons to get him to sin against me in that way.

I also picked men or was attracted to men who were already like that. The bitterroot expectancy worked both ways against me, causing me to be attracted to men who were already like that and pulling that behavior out of men who were not.

This is just one example of the ways we get bad fruit from a bad root. The bad root is the judgment against our parent(s), and the bad fruit is the behavior the expectancy produces.

How do you fix this? To put it simply, you pray through it.

The most specific prayer is to acknowledge, "I have judged." The Bible is very, very clear about judgments. It says, "Judge not lest you be judged" of the same thing.

When you judge father or mother, that judgment activates a universal law and will come back on you (often multiplied a hundred-fold and usually for several generations). A judgment against parents multiplies (because of the universal, biblical laws of sowing and reaping) and comes back with a vengeance.

Honor your father and mother is the first commandment with a promise. You find it in Exodus20:12 "Honor your father and mother so your days will be long upon the earth and things will go well with you." So, if things are not going well with you—in any area of your life, that means you haven't honored your father and mother in some way, most likely by judging them.

Judging Your Parents: A Case Study

As I've shared, that's how it worked for me. I did not honor my father, I judged him, and therefore I was reaping the consequences of my judgments of him, and by extension, all men.

How do you pray through that?

First, you've got to forgive your father, your mother, or whoever it is. You speak to them just like they are right there in front of you. In my case, "Dad, I forgive you for being unfaithful to Mom, for being an adulterer." However, it comes up in your heart, in your spirit. That's why you must forgive them. That's number one.

Before we go further, let me say this: forgiveness doesn't have to come out of your emotions. in fact, it usually doesn't. **Forgiveness is an act of your *will*.**

You are choosing to forgive someone because it's the right thing to do. You may not FEEL LIKE you have forgiven. Your feelings might not line up for a while.

After we've prayed forgiveness prayers, you have to ask the Lord to accomplish—or work—forgiveness in you. That means that once you choose to forgive somebody, the Lord will begin to work the feelings out in you. You'll start to see that you are just as guilty as the next person, and you'll realize you need and want forgiveness too.

Next, after you have forgiven your parent(s), you ask God to forgive you for judging your parents. The Bible teaches that if you don't forgive, God's not going to forgive you. You want to forgive so that you'll be forgiven. That's a universal law.

Forgiving and being forgiven end the universal Biblical laws of sowing and reaping, judging and multiplication, in your life.

CHAPTER 5

Prayer to End Bitter Root Expectations

Remember, negative patterns don't end with judgments. Those judgments create psychological expectancies (bitter root expectancies) in your subconscious that pull the behavior you judged in your parents out of other people toward you.

The judgments create a bitter psychological expectation that that is how life will go, and that is the fruit that you experience in your life. Those negative patterns keep cropping up while you wonder why this keeps happening to you.

You get rid of those bitterroot expectancies in much the same way you do the judgments that created them. You pray through it.

Here is how (and I will continue to use myself as an example):

"I renounce, as sin, the bitter root expectation that men or husbands are always unfaithful to their wives, or all men are womanizers," or something that applies to your situation and the judgments you have made against your parent(s).

Next, say, "Jesus, please reap on the cross all these seeds I've sown."

What is happening here is we are **doing business at the Cross.** We are saying, "I have this bitter root expectation, and I've planted these seeds, and they've come up, and I want them to have crop failure and stop bearing fruit in my life, so I quit reaping the consequences."

As the prayer minister, once the counselee has prayed the above, I pray, "Lord, plow up all this ground in [insert name] life, render those seeds dead and lifeless and reseed them with the truth of Your word."

That takes care of that bitterroot and its expectancy.

However, there are other ways people respond, besides just judgments and bitter root expectancies, to situations that happened to them as children.

In the next chapter, I will share another one of the ways of responding that builds negative patterns in your life, one that I did myself—inner vows.

CHAPTER 6

Inner Vows

In my healing story, one of the wrong responses I had to my father's infidelity was that I not only judged him, but I also made the leap to a blanket judgment of all men. I made the judgment that all men were going to be unfaithful and adulterers; and that women were the good, faithful ones in relationships (that's the unspoken part of that blanket judgment).

Besides the judgment against my father and all men and the bitterroot (psychological) expectancies created in me, I had another response. I made an inner vow, often also called an inner determination.

I made the inner vow that "I will never be like that. I'm never going to be unfaithful." In other words, "I'm going to be the good one. I am not going to be unfaithful." It can take any shape or form, but most often starts with the statement, "I will always," or "I will never.."

An inner vow, or an inner determination, is a negative, or sometimes even a positive, vow that you make inside your heart. Often you don't even say it out loud, but it becomes an entrenched belief system you cannot change.

The problem with inner vows is, they can put you over in the ditch on either side of the road. It can make you good, like in my case, "I'm going to be faithful, I'm not going to be the bad ones, and never cheat," etc. Or, it can put you over in the total opposite category, where you then become the adulterer and the cheater.

So, you can reap either positive or negative fruit from inner vows. Most people don't understand why good fruit from an inner vow is a bad thing. Isn't good behavior good fruit?

Inner vows lock you into behaviors and keep you from being free to make your own decisions without having that vow influence you.

They take away your free will to choose the correct action. That entrenched belief system becomes a trap that keeps you locked into a behavior pattern and doesn't leave room for God to give you other choices for new, good behaviors. You aren't free to obey God or let him lead you in new ways. You can only follow the vow.

I read a story about Kenneth Hagin (a pioneering pastor of the faith movement) and inner vows. He was new to ministry and pastoring and didn't know what to call it.

He'd come to pastor a new church, and a young man in the church had just died. Pastor Hagin went to the funeral, and as he was walking in, he said to the Lord, "Okay, God, I'll raise him from the dead if You want me to," and the Lord said, "No, things were put into motion a long time ago that cannot be reversed." Pastor Hagin had no idea what that meant. Still, as he was visiting with people and family and friends of the young man who had died (the young man was not yet thirty, or just turned thirty, something to that effect), several friends kept saying,

"Yeah, so-and-so always said he didn't want to live past thirty. He wanted to die before he was thirty. Thirty was just too old to live."

Suddenly, the Lord nudged Kenneth Hagin and said, "See?" Since Kenneth Hagin was in the faith movement, he took it as "this young man's words determined his life." This is true, and that is part of it, but it was really an inner vow. He did not want to live past thirty."

Another example of a common inner vow that I've come across often is when I've ministered to women who had abortions when they were very, very young. Invariably, after they have had the abortion, they will say, "I'll never do that again."

Often what happens is that "never" (remember, an inner vow is most often characterized by a "never," "always," or "all" statement) is made the woman's spirit, soul, and body hear that word "never" and clamp down.

If a woman has an abortion and she says in her heart, "I'll never do that again," her body "hears," We can't get ever pregnant again," or "We can never have sex again," or however it's interpreted. But most of the people I've ministered to have said when they've made that inner determination or inner vow, they have not been able to get pregnant again after that, even if they want a baby— after they are married.

This is how forceful inner vows (or inner determinations) are. With that said, it is simple to break them.

CHAPTER 7

Prayer to Break Inner Vows

How do you break an inner vow once it's been made and set and motion?

It's straightforward.

First, you have to ask the Lord to help you remember how you worded it.

Next, you must break the inner vow **out loud.**

For me it was, "I renounce as sin the inner judgment that all men are bad and unfaithful and adulterers and that all women are good. I break the inner vow and inner determination I will never be like my father and be a cheater and an adulteress, in the Name of Jesus."

If you are not sure that you've gotten the exact words, you CAN just pray it as it comes up in your heart.

Then as the prayer counselor, I will pray and ask the Lord, "Lord, sever from this person all the fruit and consequences of these inner vows, in the Name of Jesus. I ask that their spirit, soul, mind, and body remember them no longer. Lord, I ask that You would release them from these vows and determinations in the Name of Jesus."

That usually takes care of that vow and its consequences. Often it will uncover and show other vows that have been made like it's a domino effect. Once you get rid of one big inner vow, other ones might surface that you will need to break as well.

Those can then be dealt with in the same way, right away.

CHAPTER 8

Rejection

Let me share another type of wrong response and work it all the way through.

Our internal wounds are not just about what happens to us, but also what we turn around and do to our spirits and our little inner child in response to that wound.

A very common scenario is one or both parents, or another important person, rejecting a child. The fruit of that rejection usually shows up later in life, in primary adult relationships.

A typical example is of a man whose father has rejected him. It plays out that every male boss, and every male friend he's ever had, rejects him at some level.

He finally lands his dream job, and the boss loves him and his work. The boss calls the man into his office, intending to give him a raise, the corner office, and a huge promotion.

The young man's dreams are about to come true. During the

meeting where the boss intends to promote him, the young man pushes all the boss' buttons and pulls the boss's bitter root expectation for rejection out of the boss toward him. The boss winds up firing him. After it is all over, the boss is like, "Wait, I don't understand what happened. I was going to promote this guy, and I wound up firing him."

There are several issues at work here, especially these two:

1. The man made a judgment (usually against his father, that then becomes a blanket judgment against all men and all men in authority), "All men reject me."

2. That judgment then creates a bitter root psychological expectancy that pulls the rejecting behavior out of his boss and friends.

BUT, there's something else in play here, too, and that is that *he has believed a lie*—that he deserves to be rejected. This lie causes rejection on every front, with everyone who fits the category in his judgment. *He has even done something to his spirit and soul*, and it has become part of his identity.

In this scenario of rejection, multiple things need prayer.

CHAPTER 9

Praying Through Rejecting Your Own Spirit

Praying through rejecting your own spirit is a multi-step process. Don't let that stop you from doing it, though. This healing prayer is as simple as all the other ones.

Let me remind you here that you need to pray all your healing prayers OUT LOUD because the Kingdom of God is voice-activated.

Using our example of the young man who was fired instead of promoted from the previous chapter, the first thing he needs to do would be to choose to forgive his father for rejecting him.

Second, he needs to ask the Lord to forgive him for judging his father for rejecting him.

The bitterroot expectation from his father is: That God (because how we view our parents is how we view God) and other people in authority – especially bosses or males in his life, are all going to reject him.

He has to say out loud, "I renounce as sin the bitter root expectation that God, other men, and people in authority are going to reject me. Lord Jesus, please reap on the Cross these seeds I've sown."

That's as far as we went before. Now, the young man needs to go further and identify how he internalized that judgment. Here is a clue: What our parents or others in authority have done to us as children, we turn around and do to ourselves, in our spirit. He will need to talk to his spirit.

As the prayer counselor, I would say, "Let's talk to our little spirits." I would say, "little Robert, or little John, or little Johnny," (whatever your parents called you— especially if you had a nickname), "will you forgive me for rejecting you?"

Because when our parents or others in authority in any way reject us, we turnaround and reject our spirit. We reject, we repress, we put our spirit down. We're not connected to our spirit any longer. You will find more often than not when you ask your spirit, "My little spirit, will you forgive me for rejecting you?" they perk right up, and you will hear them or see them in your mind's eye, and they will say, "Yes, of course."

Sometimes, however, they won't. If your little spirit person doesn't forgive you right away, it's because they've been very, very wounded. But you need to persist and ask them to forgive you for whatever you've done to them. Maybe you've tamped them down or repressed them. Perhaps you've gagged them to silence them. Whatever it is you've done, you need to ask them to forgive you.

Once your little spirit says, "Yes, I forgive you," then you need

Praying Through Rejecting Your Own Spirit

to ask the Lord to forgive you for doing that to yourself, to the person He made you be. Because you have rejected who He made you. Say, "Lord, please forgive me for rejecting or tamping down or gagging or repressing my spirit, the person You made me."

You also have to ask the Lord to demolish the operative forces and renounce them as sin in your life. These are the forces of you rejecting yourself, gagging yourself, repressing yourself, whatever structures that you've built around your spirit that keeps it repressed, and ask the Lord to demolish those structures of rejection and repression of your spirit, in the name of Jesus, to get you out of that pattern.

CHAPTER 10

Identity Issues

The damage we do to our spirit does not stop with us doing what was done to us. It goes deeper and causes identity issues and shame issues.

First, we need to define the difference between guilt and shame.

Guilt is the feeling you have when you have done something wrong, and you know you've done something wrong, and you need to repent or change and do something else.

Shame (otherwise known as false guilt) is the feeling you have when guilt has been imputed to you, and *you did not do anything to deserve it.*

It takes listening to the Holy Spirit to get clear on the difference for you because of childhood wounds. We all have things we've done and feel guilt for (that's good), but some things we feel shame about things we have NOT done, because someone made us feel guilty even though we aren't (that's NOT good).

Let's go back to our example of the young man to see how this works.

First, we prayed that he would accept his spirit. You can find that in the previous chapter.

We have to look at the fact that our parents tell us lies by their actions and their inactions. In this young man's life, he was told a lie by his father's actions or inactions, that he deserved to be rejected or was not worth having a relationship.

Most often, this shows up as an "I deserve rejection" statement. That lie, "I deserve rejection," becomes a profound identity issue for this young man. So much so, his core identity becomes, "I deserve rejection. I must be rotten. I must be terrible."

Because we act out of our core identity, the young man will do things that cause people to think of him that way. And this identity issue will progress and get worse and worse and worse until people believe that he is terrible. He may have even become the horrible person deserving of rejection he believes he is.

What can he do? It's another case of going back so he can go forward. He has to go back and forgive his father to tell him the lie that he deserves rejection and that he did not deserve to have a relationship with the dad.

Then he must ask the Lord to forgive him ("forgive me") for judging his dad for telling him that lie through actions and inactions.

But there is one more step. We have to come out of agreement with the lie. This is how we pray through coming out of agreement with the lie (remember this is done out loud):

Identity Issues

> "I come out of agreement with the lie that my father told me by his actions and inactions (name them specifically if you can) that I deserve rejection, that I'm not good enough to have a relationship (or however it comes up for the young man in his spirit and his heart), and I come out of agreement with you Dad, and with anyone else that believed that lie and I come out of agreement with everyone else that believes that lie."

That's the first part of coming out of agreement with the lie.

The second part is, you have to come out of agreement with Satan, who's the father of all lies, and your accuser. So, you pray out loud,

> "I come out of agreement with Satan, who's the Father of all lies, especially this lie *and* my accuser."

Next, you have to ask the Lord to forgive you for **believing the lie.**

Pray out loud:

> "Lord, forgive me for believing that lie, and I repent for believing that lie. Jesus break the power of that lie in me and over me and establish Your truth in its place."

As the minster, I now pray:

> "Lord, as far as that lie has gone in their spirit, soul, and body, Lord take it out, take it out, do what You have to do."

At this point, I ask the Holy Spirit / the Lord, however, you want to word it, to tell the person—in this case, the young man suffering from an identity of rejection, the truth: this is the lie that's (name the lie).

Then I pray:

> "Lord, tell Your truth about [insert me/your name]."

At this point, you need to sit and wait quietly until the Lord speaks to your heart—who He says you are. When you hear that in your heart, and it's resounding, then you need to take communion on that truth. You need to take the body and the blood of Jesus and receive what the Lord has said about you.

Then you need to pray for every time someone told you that lie in your life. Ask the Holy Spirit to go back in time; cleanse your timeline of shame, guilt, false guilt, defilement of the lie that has been perpetuated, and cleanse the memory of that lie from your spirit, soul, and body, and all your memories in Jesus' name.

This is how to pray through shame and identity issues that come from the lies you have believed that have kept you bound.

CHAPTER 11

Soul Ties

The last pillar of inner healing is soul ties.

Soul ties happen when we have deep relationships with other people. They can be emotional and mental/psychological, but they are often sexual-formed through sexual relationships.

The Bible is clear: when you have sex with someone, you become one with them, spirit, soul, and body. Not only that, you become one with every other person they have had sex with, which begins to make a highly complex web of ties.

I heard Kelly Copeland (daughter of Kenneth Copeland) say years ago that she wished she had known as a teenager and beginning to date how much each person she dated would change her.

Invariably, you want to please the other person, which changes you and creates a bond with them. Changing for another person you are dating is one of the mildest forms of a soul tie.

If you create deep soul ties with someone, especially by having sex with them, you become one with them.

This is a great mystery, but this is what the Bible says: when you have sex with someone, you "know" them. The Hebrew word is "yadah"—which means to know a person in the most profound, most intimate way and become one with them—their good, bad, and ugly.

And usually, it's the bad and the ugly that sticks to us, unfortunately.

You have to separate and sever yourself from the people that you have been intimately involved with by prayer,

whether that is physically, sexually, or emotionally/mentally.

There is another level of soul ties: allowing other people to control you, whether you have sex with them or not. This level of soul tie involves giving other people control over you, giving your will over to them to control you.

CHAPTER 12

Sample Prayers to Break Soul Ties

Here is a sample prayer for you to pray for release from sexual soul ties—from anyone you have had sex with (or even sexual behavior without intercourse). Remember, you need to pray these out loud:

> "Lord Jesus, I confess that I have engaged sexually outside the bounds of your Word and Your laws with _____ (insert the names of the people you have been sexually intimate within the blank).
>
> "I accept the complete responsibility for each of these acts of sin and admit I committed them as an act of my will. I know that engaging in sexual acts before or outside of marriage is sin and that I have broken Your universal laws and deserve to realize the consequences of my actions.
>
> "I ask that you would forgive me for disobeying You and Your Commandments, that you would cleanse me by the Blood of Jesus, and set me and my generations free from all the consequences, bondages, and curses that come from disobeying

and breaking Your laws.

(This next portion is for those you've sexually engaged with.)

"Please give your grace, mercy, and blessing to (insert the names of the people you have engaged with sexually and their descendants in the blank) _____. Set them free from the consequences, bondages, and curses that have come on them from disobeying and breaking Your laws and sinning against You. I release _____ (insert the names) into Your care spirit, soul, and body, in thought word, and deed. Forgive me for the harm that I've caused them and their descendants.

"By my free will, I gave myself in a sexual relationship to _____ (insert names of sexual partners). According to Your Word, the Bible, I became one with them and entered into an intimate, covenant relationship with them before You. I turn from and repent for my willful disobedience and sinful acts.

"Now, I choose to come into alignment with Your Word, the Bible, and obey your commands concerning sexual purity.

"I come out of agreement with every covenant, union, bond, tie, and agreement that I made through engaging with each of them sexually. I sever and annul every covenant, union, bond, tie, and agreement created between each of them and me. Jesus, I ask that You would break the power of these bonds in me and over me.

"I put the Cross and resurrection power of Jesus Christ between

Sample Prayers to Break Soul Ties

me and everyone with whom I have sexually sinned. Jesus, please cleanse me from all defilement, the memory, and even the scent of my sin. I ask that You would place anything transferred between me and those I sinned with onto the Cross.

"Please close every door or portal of access that I opened to the enemy or the demonic realm through my sin. Please deliver me of all evil that may have passed through these open doors and from those I sinned with to me. I ask you to send your angels to escort any demonic guards, familiar spirits, or higher levels of spiritual darkness that I may have given access to my life through these open doors.

"Jesus, deliver me from any forces of darkness that gained access to my life through this sin and the soul ties it formed. In the name of Jesus, I resist the devil and any entity that does not bow the knee to Jesus, and I take authority over the spirits tormenting me.

After you've prayed the above prayers, it is an excellent time to take a few moments and see if there's any spirit of lust, or homosexuality, or adultery, or other dark spirits tormenting you. If you feel there are, pray this next:

"In the name of Jesus, I take authority over you spirit of _____ (lust, homosexuality, etc.) and I command your power and hold over me to be broken, and that you leave me now, forever.

"Jesus, please cleanse me and set me free from the shame that has had me in bondage—my shame and the shame that others have put on me. Restore the honor and dignity that are my rightful inheritance as Your beloved child to me. I ask that You return to me all that is rightfully mine, cleansed and restored through the Blood of Jesus, transferred from me to those I have sinned with.

"Please heal my spirit, soul, and body, and restore any portion of my spirit or soul that was fragmented, broken, or torn back to the condition You designed for it.

Heal my heart and guard it by Your power and love.

"Lord, restore me to my original, Divine design, the person you created me to be. Romans 12:2 says to "be transformed by the renewing of your mind." I ask that you renew my mind and collect all loose ends that I may have and make me whole, spirit, soul, and body.

"I choose to disconnect from every way I connected with these people, and I choose now to connect with You in every way so that I can love You as You commanded: with all my heart, with all my soul, with all my mind, and all my strength.

"Holy Spirit, pass the Sword of the Spirit between me and this person/these people and sever all ties between us: physically, mentally, spiritually, emotionally, sexually, financially- every single tie in every area.

"I call back everything they took from me cleansed and restored from all defilement. I send back to this person anything I took from them, cleansed and restored from all defilement in Jesus' name. Lord, please completely separate us in the Name of Jesus.

Sample Prayers to Break Soul Ties

Amen.

Here is a sample prayer to break the Soul Ties of Control. The final prayer to break soul ties is the prayer to be released from control's soul ties. Fill in the blanks with the names of people that you have allowed to control you. The issue of control can go back into your childhood and forward into adulthood. Parents, teachers, leaders, girlfriends and boyfriends, husbands, wives, ex-husbands and ex-wives, your children, even credit card companies, banks, and governments are all possible sources of control in your life.

Whatever the source of control the Lord brings up, that is what you need to break the soul ties of control.

Again, this is a sample prayer. You'll insert the names of the people you have allowed to control you in the blanks. After you've prayed this prayer, if you think of someone, later on, ask the Lord to do a supplement to your prayer, breaking the soul tie of control. (e.g., "I'd like to add this person to the prayer as well.")

Remember: These prayers must be prayed out loud.

Sample prayer for release from soul ties of control:

"Lord Jesus, I confess that I have allowed (insert names of those you have allowed to control you) _____ to control me. I am fully responsible for giving over my will to these people and placed them in a position of domination and power over my life.

"Thank for You for Your mercy and grace. Please forgive me and cleanse me of this sin of allowing someone other than You to have control over my life and for surrendering my will to someone other than You. I forgive each of them, and I sever and come out of agreement with every union, bond, agreement, and tie that I have made with them.

"In the name of Jesus Christ, I break the power of all unions, bonds, agreements, and ties. Jesus set me and my generations free from any effects, curses, and consequences that have been activated against us by any soul tie of control.

"Jesus, set me free from any covenant agreement, whether written, verbal, or implied that I have made with each of these persons.

"I embrace the new covenant of your Blood, Jesus, through the Cross that annuls, overrules, repudiates, and sets aside every other covenant or agreement.

"In Jesus' name I put the Cross, the Blood, Holy Spirit, between each of these people and me and commit them into Your hands—spirit, soul, body, thought, word, action.

"Cleanse me from anything I have taken from this relationship, and I take back anything that was stolen from me, cleansed through the Blood of Jesus. Jesus, gather up all my loose ends and rebuild me and reestablish me to Your original design, the person you have created me to be from the foundations of the world.

"Restore my discernment, my conscience, and my ability to hear You through the voice of Holy Spirit.

Sample Prayers to Break Soul Ties

"Forgive me for yielding my will to another human being. I say that You are my only Lord and Savior. I choose to yield my will only to You, Lord, from this moment forward.

"Rebuild, reinforce, and strengthen my inner man—my spirit and my will. Give me Your wisdom, knowledge, and understanding so I can choose Your ways from this from today forward.

"I renounce all authority, manipulation, domination, or control that has been exerted over me by these people.

"I break all covenants, pacts, promises, curses, and every other work of darkness that I have been exposed to or made liable to my actions or the actions of others.

"By the decision of my own will, I cut myself free from every soul tie and every form of bondage of my spirit, soul, or body to satan or any sentient creature that does not bow the knee to Jesus Christ.

"I present my body as a living sacrifice to the Lord as the scripture commands. I choose to walk from this moment forward in holiness as You, Lord, empower me to do so.

"Bring to light and heal the wounds that made me susceptible to these soul ties. Please reveal any sin, judgment, inner vow, or lie that allowed this soul tie to become entrenched in my life.

"As I now submit to You, Lord, and resist the enemy as Your Word commands, deliver me from any force of darkness that gained a foothold in my life, through my sin or these soul ties.

"Send angels to escort away any force of darkness that oppresses, hinders, or affects me.

"Sever all bonds that give these people or any spirit of darkness access to me or my generations.

"I choose to entirely and fully detach and disconnect from these people in every way. I completely and fully connect to You Jesus in every way so that I can love You with all my heart, soul, mind, and strength as Your Word commands.

"Thank you for delivering me. In Jesus' name, Amen

CONCLUSION

After praying through these areas that need healing in your life from this book, it is always good to ask the Holy Spirit to seal the work done in your heart.

That means that the work that has been accomplished will not be lost or forgotten; that God's Word and His healing and deliverance will have a free course in your spirit, soul, and your body from this moment forward.

As I wrote at the beginning of the book, these are just the four basics of inner healing. I've just given you a few examples of what they might look like in your life. Don't be afraid to substitute other things in there. The wounds and how you reacted to them could take any number of different forms.

I've dealt with many people, even siblings from the same family, that grew up in the same set of circumstances, but their experiences were different because *it's not so much what happens to you, but how you perceive it, and more importantly, how you respond to it.*

My brother and I grew up in the same circumstances but how we responded was very different. We had different sinful responses to the same things that happened to us and had different bad fruit.

Don't assume that your siblings (or other people in your family) had the same perception or reaction to an experience because you reacted to one experience in a certain way. Or, that you should have the same response as someone else in your family.

Everyone's response to events is different. Now, let's get to the best part, the blessing!

> *"I bless you now to allow the Lord to go deep into your inner man and bring great freedom and great healing to your spirit, soul, and your body, in Jesus' name.*

Made in United States
Orlando, FL
29 May 2022